A souvenir guide

Bodnant Garden
Conwy

Fran Llewellyn

National Trust

Heaven on Earth

Hewn out of a hillside in North Wales is Bodnant Garden, a Grade I-listed horticultural paradise forged by the Victorian vision of one extraordinary man – Henry Pochin – perfected by his descendants and today cherished by visitors the world over.

The garden's 32 hectares (80 acres) drop dramatically from manicured lawns and grand, flower-filled terraces, through buzzing wildflower meadows and pastoral glades, into an awe-inspiring dell of waterfalls and towering trees. Founded in 1874 and cared for by the National Trust since 1949, Bodnant is a garden of firsts – home to Britain's earliest and grandest laburnum arch, to new plant species discovered by botanical explorers, and to unique plant hybrids which have been born and bred here. Exotic trees, shrubs and flowers from the Andes to the Himalayas have made their home in the Snowdonia foothills, providing a year-round spectacle of garden creativity.

Bodnant is also a deeply personal garden, as much about secluded nooks as grand panoramas. It is a place to escape, to explore, to become immersed in nature and to create lasting memories.

Above all the story of Bodnant Garden is about people – the vision of those who created it, the botanical passion of those who filled it with plants, the skill of those who have cultivated it through 140 years ... and the joy of those who visit.

Left Pergola urn with the inscription Nefoedd ar Ddaear ('Heaven on Earth') – erected in 2014 to mark the centenary of the garden terraces and the outbreak of the First World War. The inscription was inspired by the words of a visitor

Right Cloudscape over mountains: a view from the Lily Terrace

Bodnant Garden's Beginnings

Bodnant Garden nestles in the Conwy Valley, four miles inland from the historic coastal town of Conwy with its imposing Edward I castle, and eight miles from the Victorian seaside resort of Llandudno.

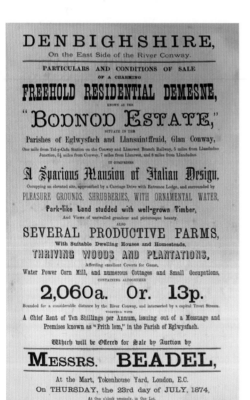

DENBIGHSHIRE,
On the East Side of the River Conway.

PARTICULARS AND CONDITIONS OF SALE
OF A CHARMING

FREEHOLD RESIDENTIAL DEMESNE,
KNOWN AS THE
"BODNOD ESTATE,"
SITUATE IN THE
Parishes of Eglwysfach and Llansaintffraid, Glan Conway,
One mile from Tal-y-Cafn Station on the Conway and Llanrwst Branch Railway, 5 miles from Llandudno
Junction, 5½ miles from Conway, 7 miles from Llanrwst, and 8 miles from Llandudno.

IT COMPRISES

A Spacious Mansion of Italian Design,
Occupying an elevated site, approached by a Carriage Drive with Entrance Lodge, and surrounded by
PLEASURE GROUNDS, SHRUBBERIES, WITH ORNAMENTAL WATER,
Park-like Land studded with well-grown Timber,
And Views of unrivalled grandeur and picturesque beauty.

ALSO

SEVERAL PRODUCTIVE FARMS,
With Suitable Dwelling Houses and Homesteads,
THRIVING WOODS AND PLANTATIONS,
Affording excellent Coverts for Game,
Water Power Corn Mill, and numerous Cottages and Small Occupations,
CONTAINING ALTOGETHER

2,060a. 0r. 13p.
Bounded for a considerable distance by the River Conway, and intersected by a capital Trout Stream.

TOGETHER WITH

A Chief Rent of Ten Shillings per Annum, issuing out of a Messuage and
Premises known as "Frith lom," in the Parish of Eglwysfach.

Which will be Offered for Sale by Auction by

MESSRS. BEADEL,
At the Mart, Tokenhouse Yard, London, E.C.
On THURSDAY, the 23rd day of JULY, 1874.
At One o'clock precisely, in One Lot.

It lies at the heart of an age-old farming community dotted with hafods (stockmen's summer dwellings) and ancient drovers' tracks. Below the surface of this peaceful, sheep-filled landscape is a rich history. Roman settlers, Dark Age Welsh princes, medieval English kings and Victorian industrialists have been drawn here by its mineral, agricultural or defensive worth … and tourists, by its beauty.

For millennia farming in this area has gone hand in hand with mining, as evidenced by the prehistoric quarrying on the Great Orme, the limestone headland near Llandudno. By the 1700s inland market towns were bustling with river traffic transporting slate, mineral ore and wool to the coast; by the 1800s the London to Holyhead Mail Coach had put Snowdonia on the Victorian tourist map and by the 1870s the Conwy Valley Railway was transporting not only freight but also a new wave of holidaymakers back and forth between coast and mountains.

'The position of Bodnant, the natural dell and its river and the view of the blue mountains sprinkled with snow in the distance, make a natural setting for a woodland garden of unparalleled beauty.'
Henry Duncan McLaren,
2nd Baron Aberconway

Dwelling by a stream

The estate of Bodnant was the home of the Lloyd family from the reign of King James I. In the mid-1700s it passed down the female line by marriage to the Forbes family and then through marriage again in 1820 to the sixth son of a baronet, William Hanmer of Bettisfield Park in Flintshire. The house was described in *A Topographical Dictionary of Wales* in 1829 as 'a handsome edifice, pleasantly situated, and commanding extensive and richly diversified views over the Vale of Conway'.

By the time industrialist Henry Davis Pochin bought the 810-hectare (2,000-acre) plot in 1874, for the grand sum of £62,500, it was an estate with a walled garden and 'pleasure grounds, shrubberies, with ornamental water and park-like land ... along with woods and plantations'. At this time it was called Bodnod – in Welsh 'bod' meaning dwelling and 'nod' meaning a prominent place. Pochin made his own mark, the first of many, reverting back to the earlier and more romantic name of Bodnant, meaning 'dwelling by a stream'.

Far left Advertisement for the sale of 'Bodnod', 1874

Left Age-old farming landscape: the Conwy Valley

Above The Georgian Bodnant Hall, landscaped park and pleasure grounds above the meandering River Conwy in the early 1800s

The Georgian landscape

Wrapped around the formal areas of the garden are native meadows and woods, and within them lie the remnants of the oldest parts of the estate – the Georgian park 'studded with well grown timber, woods and plantations'.

The Old Park

Unfolding beyond the southern edge of the formal garden is the Old Park, a pretty meadow with mature native trees. The parkland was laid out by John Forbes in 1792 who built an Italianate mansion to replace an earlier house. The front of his classical, white-stuccoed house with its sweeping driveway faced south, overlooking an artistically crafted, pastoral view.

Forbes was influenced by the English Landscape style which sought to recreate an idealised countryside akin to paintings of the day. It was a style developed during the 18th century by landscape designers such as William Kent, 'Capability' Brown and Humphry Repton, and brought nature close to the house with a subtle panorama of rolling grassland, groupings of native trees and grazing livestock. A ditch or ha-ha kept cows and sheep away from the lawns and flower beds and out of the kitchen garden. The ha-ha's stone retaining wall provided an effective barrier while remaining invisible from the house.

In this period many of the oak, sycamore and beech trees around the estate were planted. Beech was uncommon in North Wales in the late 18th century – Bodnant's owner was keeping pace with contemporary landscaping trends.

For more than two centuries the Old Park was closed to everyone but gardeners and livestock and has quietly aged into a species-rich wildflower meadow. It was opened to the public in 2012 and today offers delightful strolls through snowdrops in winter, daffodils in spring, wild flowers and grasses in summer and dazzling views of tree colour in autumn.

Above left The temple on top of the Heather Hill – one of the best seats in the garden

Above A carpet of daffodils in the Old Park

The Heather Hill

Overlooking the Old Park is the Heather Hill. On top of this heather-clad mound is a classical-style temple which pays homage to the romantic follies of the English Landscape movement. It is in fact a modern reproduction, built in Italy and made of limestone with a wrought-iron dome. It was bought from a dealer and erected at Bodnant Garden in 1980s by Charles McLaren, 3rd Baron Aberconway, and his wife Ann. Looking out westwards across the Old Park to the River Conwy and Carneddau Mountains, the mound provides some of the best views of the original garden and its beautiful valley setting.

A working estate

Lying on the western fringes of the garden and along the west bank of the River Hiraethlyn is Furnace Hill. The wood here contains native trees as well as imported specimens planted from Victorian times. Water and timber from these two natural features have fuelled life on the estate for centuries.

A mill race, or leat, runs alongside the river. Believed to be Tudor in origin, it would have served the blast furnace nearby – which gave its name to the area. Estate records also describe a leat, river and dam upstream powering a mill in the late 1700s. The present building, from the late Georgian period, was a flour mill; later, it was extended and became a sawmill.

Below Furnace Meadow in summer

Meadows and woodland

As well as being a home for exotic trees and shrubs, today Furnace Hill is a haven for wildlife and a perfect place for garden bird walks, bat-spotting and bug hunts. Next to the wood is Furnace Meadow, a grassland rich in wildlife.

Bodnant Garden has a management plan for all its grasslands – the Old Park, Furnace Meadow and also Cae Poeth Meadow to the north of the garden (see page 52). This involves low-level annual maintenance – cutting grass and removing the hay in August, grazing the land with sheep in the autumn, and collecting and sowing the seeds of particular wildflower species, such as yellow rattle, to help them flourish. Just as important, the National Trust is extending access to the meadows so visitors can enjoy relaxed strolls, guided nature trails and even scything workshops.

Gardeners are hard at work preparing Furnace Hill and Meadow, and Cae Poeth Meadow, for opening to the public in the near future.

The Old Mill

The Old Mill is now a Grade II-listed building. It was built between 1828 and 1837 by William Hanmer, in the classical Italian style. It was out-of-use by around 1900 and while some of the original workings, showing fine craftsmanship, remain inside, the building has been derelict for many years. Picturesque but redundant, it awaits funding for restoration.

In 2013 the wheel house was opened to the public, allowing visitors to view the large wheel inside. In the same year volunteers cleared, cleaned and refurbished part of the building to create a cosy indoor space. This is now used for family craft workshops, talks and demonstrations, and provides refreshments and a seating area in winter.

Left View from the Dell of the Old Mill, at the foot of the wooded Furnace Hill

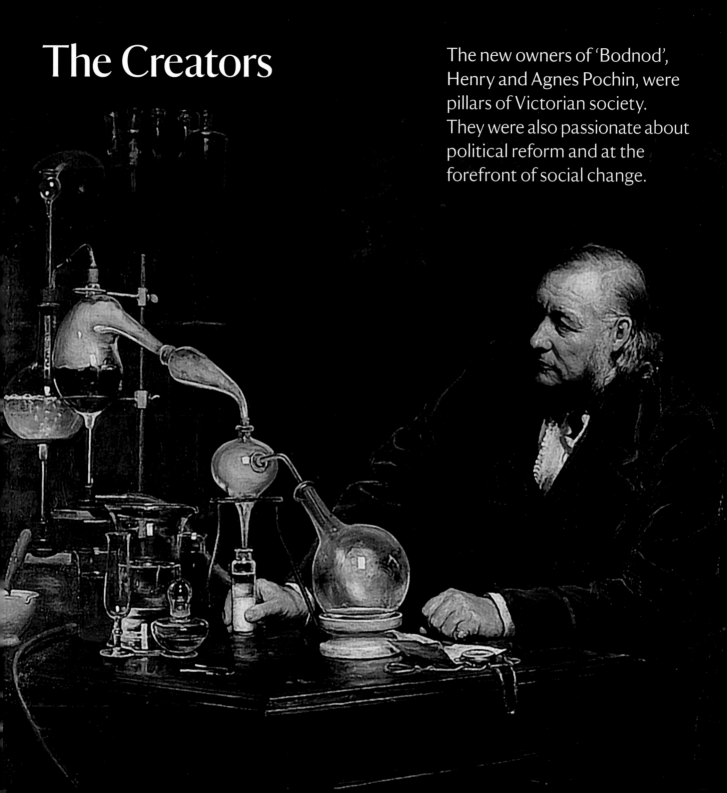

The Creators

The new owners of 'Bodnod',
Henry and Agnes Pochin, were
pillars of Victorian society.
They were also passionate about
political reform and at the
forefront of social change.

Henry Davis Pochin was born in 1824, the son of a yeoman farmer from Leicestershire. Following a pharmaceutical apprenticeship he became partner in a firm of chemists in Manchester called James Woolley. Pochin quickly made his name, and fortune, with two big ideas: one was a distillation process to turn soap – until that time brown in colour – to white; the other was the production of alum cake, in great demand in the paper-making and dyeing industry. With growing profits and industrial connections emerged Henry Pochin, the financier. In 1862 he led a Manchester syndicate to float new limited companies in the coal, iron and steel, engineering and shipbuilding industries.

Industrious urban life

Henry Pochin was also an aspiring politician with radical Liberal leanings and in 1852 he married Agnes Heap, who was at the forefront of the campaign for women's suffrage in Manchester.

The couple were active in their community of Salford, improving conditions for working men and women and providing relief during the cotton famine of the 1860s. As councillor and mayor, Pochin worked to bring gas lights to all homes, to improve sanitation and reduce overcrowding. He also founded the Salford Free Library and Museum and a Working Men's College, while his wife Agnes established a school for girls.

The Pochins achieved great things in Manchester but it was a time of personal tragedy too; they lost four of their six children along the way. Henry stood for parliament in 1865 and 1868, but by 1871 he was looking towards a country life in North Wales and finally bought the estate of Bodnod in 1874.

A country retirement

With his typical vigour Henry Pochin the landowner set about remodelling the house and garden, building cottages on the estate and improving farming practices. He also bought land at nearby Prestatyn, where he supplied the seaside town with gas and clean water, built flood defences and developed a foreshore with a promenade. He went on to become a JP, Deputy Lieutenant and High Sheriff of Denbighshire.

Still active in business during the 1880s, Pochin became Director of the Metropolitan Railway Company but was beset by ill health in later life and died in 1895, Agnes surviving him until 1908. Throughout her life she continued to write and lecture on women's rights, helping to found the Manchester Society for Women's Suffrage in 1868 and the National Union of Women's Suffrage Societies in 1897.

Sadness had overshadowed the Pochins' family life. Their surviving son Percival was disinherited following an unsuitable marriage and a court case involving the mistreatment of a servant. Their daughter, Laura, inherited the estate on her father's death. It was a great gift, and passed into good hands.

Opposite *'The Chemist' – Henry Davis Pochin* by 19th-century portrait painter Walter William Ouless (RA)

Below from left Henry Davis Pochin, Mayor of Salford, and Agnes Pochin, writer and campaigner for women's suffrage during the 1860s

A great gift

Laura shared her father's passion for the garden as did her son, Henry Duncan McLaren. Together they built on the foundations Henry Pochin had laid. Laura was a lover of herbaceous plants, roses and peonies, as well as native flora. She developed the wild garden of the Far End after her father's death and made plans for the Italianate terraces with her son.

Laura inherited her parents' political drive. In 1877 she married barrister Charles Benjamin Bright McLaren, MP for Stafford and Bosworth and nephew of John Bright the famed Liberal politician. She carried the baton for women's rights after her mother, serving on the committee of the London National Society of Women's Suffrage.

Above Henry and Christabel McLaren with King George and Queen Mary at Chelsea Flower Show in 1931

Below Laura Pochin and Charles Benjamin Bright McLaren, pictured in their youth (c.1870s)

Charles McLaren took on his father-in-law's many companies which included the Tredegar Iron and Coal Company, English China Clays, the Metropolitan Railway Company and a shipbuilding firm, John Brown and Company. He was made a peer in 1911 and chose the title Lord Aberconway (meaning 'mouth of the Conwy River'). While the McLarens' business and political life kept them in London, Laura handed the care of the garden to her son Henry on his leaving Oxford University in 1901, aged 21. From the Edwardian period the McLarens moved in high horticultural circles and entertained famous figures of the day such as Ellen Willmott at Bodnant Garden. Laura's youngest son Francis was also related through marriage to Gertrude Jekyll.

In later years Laura went on to develop her celebrated garden at the Château de la Garoupe in the south of France, where she died in 1933 (followed a year later by her husband). Laura was described in her obituary in *The Times* as one of the greatest horticulturists in Europe.

A great love

In 1910 Laura's son Henry married Christabel Macnaghten, a society beauty and patron of the arts, and together they had five children. Following in his father's footsteps Henry was Liberal MP for West Staffordshire and Bosworth and served as Private Under-Secretary to David Lloyd George when he was the President of the Board of Trade. Henry left politics in 1922 but continued to lead his father's and grandfather's many companies, also inheriting the title of 2nd Baron Aberconway.

Henry's great love was Bodnant Garden, to which he devoted more than 50 years of his life. His crowning achievement was the construction of the five terraces between 1904 and 1914.

While his mother's love had been decorative flowers, Henry's passion was for the exotic new trees, shrubs and herbaceous plants being discovered in Asia and the Americas. He was also keenly interested in propagation and hybridising and was a frequent visitor to Bodnant's glasshouses.

Henry was active in showing plants at Chelsea Flower Show, winning many gold medals, and he was President of the Royal Horticultural Society (RHS) from 1931 until his death in 1953. In 1948 he also persuaded the National Trust to begin accepting exceptional gardens.

'No words can express how great a gift that was, and during her [my mother's] lifetime she and I gardened in this garden together and I myself after her death, making it much what it is today.'

Henry Duncan McLaren, RHS Journal, 1950

Below The McLarens at Bodnant Hall (c.1905); a widowed Anges Pochin (seated) with daughter Laura and Charles McLaren – Lord and Lady Aberconway – beside her. Also pictured are Laura and Charles's family (from left): Francis McLaren, Florence McLaren (and husband Sir Henry Norman), Elsie McLaren (and husband Sir Edward Johnson-Ferguson) and Henry Duncan McLaren (second from right)

Five generations

Henry's son Charles McLaren was devoted to the garden at Bodnant from a young age and fondly recalled helping his father set up flower show exhibits.

He went into the family businesses, including the shipbuilders, John Brown and Company, which, during the 1930s, built the liners *Queen Mary* and *Queen Elizabeth*. His role as a young captain of industry led him to take part in a secret meeting of leading British businessmen with Hermann Göring in August 1939 in an eleventh-hour bid to prevent war. That effort having failed, Charles went on to serve in the Royal Artillery.

After Dunkerque he worked at Westland, which built Lysander aircraft that dropped agents into France. After the war he became a JP and High Sheriff of Denbighshire in 1948 and 1950. When Henry McLaren died in 1953 Charles inherited the title of 3rd Baron Aberconway and with it the care of Bodnant Estate and Garden.

Above Michael and Caroline McLaren (left) with horticulturalist and broadcaster Christine Walkden at the opening of the Far End in 2015

Roles of honour

Over the next 50 years, Charles and his wife Ann continued to develop Bodnant Garden for the National Trust, making improvements, opening new vistas and adding new plants. In 1974 he supplemented his father's endowment to Bodnant with a gift of £131,000.

Charles won many Royal Horticultural Society prizes for his camellias and rhododendrons, on which he was an authority. Like his father, he served as President of the RHS (from 1961 until 1984) and became well known for his annual declaration, 'I think I can say, without fear of contradiction, that this is the finest Chelsea Flower Show ever.'

He presided over many garden shows and festivals and, like his father and grandmother before him, was awarded the Victoria Medal of Honour, the highest accolade given by the RHS.

Charles and Ann's son, Michael McLaren, inherited the estate in 2003 on his father's death. A practising QC, Michael and his wife Caroline are keenly involved to this day, maintaining the family's historic and creative links to the garden. As Director of Bodnant Garden, Michael has an input in all major developments and restoration projects.

For ever, for everyone

In 1948 Henry McLaren persuaded the National Trust to accept gardens, not just those attached to great houses, into the fold. His proposal was hotly debated within the Trust but was finally accepted on the basis that 'only gardens of great beauty, gardens of outstanding design or historic interest' would be considered and those having 'collections of plants or trees of value to the nation'.

A man of deeds as well as words, Henry gifted Bodnant Garden to the National Trust in 1949, so that it would 'always remain a joy and an inspiration to garden lovers'. It was given with a large private endowment, the deed of gift allowing Henry and his heirs to maintain their involvement in the garden. Bodnant Hall and Bodnant Estate remain in the McLaren family to this day.

Left **Charles McLaren, 3rd Lord Aberconway, by Michael Noakes RA, 1980s**

Above **Charles and Ann Aberconway meeting the late Queen Mother on her visit to Bodnant Garden in 1965**

The plant hunters

Key to the development of Bodnant Garden were the discoveries of famous planthunters of the 19th and 20th centuries – men who risked life and limb scouring inhospitable regions of the globe to bring back never-before-seen trees, shrubs and flowers to Britain.

It is thanks to these intrepid adventurers that Bodnant Garden is home to such a diverse plant collection. Seeds of collected plants were nurtured by new nurseries and planted in parks and gardens by Victorian landowners. Henry Pochin was keen to display these new discoveries and wasted no time in planting North American pines and redwoods in The Dell.

In the early 20th century the garden entered a second phase of plant introduction which brought a new influx of trees, shrubs and herbaceous plants, particularly from Asia. Henry McLaren was an active sponsor of botanical expeditions and even travelled to India himself in 1927.

Right A legacy of plant hunters – American conifers reach skywards and Asian rhododendrons cloak the hillside at Bodnant Garden

Far right Hand-coloured illustration of *Rhododendron arboreum*, drawn and engraved by William Clark (fl.1820s)

Opposite top Sponsored by Henry, 2nd Lord Aberconway, plant hunters such as George Forrest brought back from Asia a new wave of rhododendrons, especially much-prized red varieties, to the gardens of Britain

The pioneers

Ernest Wilson collected in China in the early 1900s. His travels furnished Bodnant Garden with magnolias and rhododendrons as well as the *Lilium regale* which were the cause of his 'Lily Limp' – he was injured in an avalanche during the expedition which led to their discovery.

In 1917 the Rhododendron Society, of which Henry McLaren was a leading member, engaged another botanist George Forrest. Forrest was already a seasoned traveller in China and had almost been killed by Buddhist lamas during the bloody Tibetan Rebellion in 1905. His expedition brought forth many new rhododendrons which caused a sensation, especially the bright reds which were rare at that time and formed the basis for Bodnant's hybridisation programme from the 1920s.

In 1925 Henry headed a group of garden owners who called themselves the Andes Syndicate; they sponsored Harold Comber to bring back new plants from the mountains of South America, including the beautiful *Embothrium coccineum* (Chilean firebush).

Throughout the 1920s and 1930s Henry also supported the expeditions of planthunters in the Himalayas: Frank Kingdon-Ward, who was the first person to send back seed of the Himalayan blue poppy; Frank Ludlow and George Sherriff, who discovered many new rhododendrons and primulas; and Joseph Rock, who survived the ferocious Communist takeover in 1949, returning with plants such as the *Paeonia rockii*, Rock's peony.

'The plant names alone will show how the temperate regions of the world from the Andes to the Himalayas and from the Blue Mountains to the Caucasus have been ransacked for good plants but they will not show how these plants have been absorbed into a great garden. Plants are after all only the raw material and to weave them into a harmonious whole is to compose a great symphony.'

Frank Kingdon-Ward,
The Gardeners' Chronicle, 1928

The gardeners

Henry McLaren was a great plantsman, but admitted he 'did not have green fingers'. Happily Bodnant Garden has been blessed with men and women not only with vision but also with great gardening skill.

When he arrived at Bodnant in 1874, Henry Pochin enlisted a leading landscape designer of the day, Edward Milner, to help create his vision. Milner was born in Derbyshire in 1819 and worked at Chatsworth as an apprentice to the head gardener, the famous Joseph Paxton. Milner went on to be Superintendent of Works for Paxton's crowning achievement, the Crystal Palace, and from there to design many public and private gardens. The latter included parks in Lancashire built to ease unemployment caused by the 'cotton famine' of the 1860s.

Milner, assisted by his son Henry, set out ambitious plans to remodel the landscape around Bodnant Hall. The man charged with the work was George Ellis who had previously been head gardener at Kirkby Mallory, an estate in Leicestershire once owned by the estranged wife of the notorious Lord Byron.

Above Head Gardener Joseph Saunderson, kneeling, assists Mr and Mrs Pochin and friends planting a tree in the new pinetum at Bodnant Garden in 1887

Ellis arrived at Bodnant with his young family in the mid-1870s. After his wife sadly died in 1881 Mr Ellis appears to have moved away, following several seminal years which shaped the garden and led to the development of the wild dells and the formal upper garden.

Establishing roots

In the early 1880s a new head gardener appears in the Bodnant record books. Like Edward Milner, Joseph Saunderson had previously worked at Chatsworth, famous for its Paxton glasshouse. Under Saunderson, Bodnant's own glasshouses and kitchen garden went on to yield prize-winning produce.

Saunderson settled at Bodnant with his family. Through his 30-year career he continued developing the dells and the upper garden, directing work on the terraces (begun in 1904), and planting the first Chinese magnolias, camellias and many other exotics. His son Eric followed him into gardening, but was killed in the First World War.

On Saunderson's retirement in 1911 the mantle of head gardener was assumed by George Gurney, from Hertfordshire. He held the role for almost a decade, throughout the difficult years of the war when many working men on the estate left to fight and did not return.

Gurney took over the massive building project of the terraces which was finished by 1914, although some additions were made after the war. Sadly Gurney died in 1920 aged just 56. An obituary in the *Gardener's Chronicle* reported: 'He was an enthusiastic and successful gardener, and passionately fond of flowers … a true patriot, loved and respected by all who knew him.'

Right Before and after: Bodnant Hall and upper grounds in 1874 (above) and Pochin's redesigned house and East Garden in the 1880s (below)

Growing the garden on

George Gurney's successor in 1920 was Frederick Puddle – and so began the most famous period in Bodnant Garden's history. For the next eight-and-a-half decades the development of the garden was a family affair, a partnership between three generations of McLarens – Henry, Charles and Michael – and three generations of Puddles – Frederick, Charles and Martin.

Frederick Puddle was head gardener during a dynamic phase of Bodnant's evolution, with the introduction of new plants from Asia and America. He was also at the forefront of the garden's plant breeding programme. A talented horticulturalist, he took Bodnant Garden to gold success at many Chelsea flower shows and was awarded the RHS Victoria Medal of Honour alongside his employer.

From 1947 Frederick's son Charles followed in his footsteps to become head gardener and was also awarded the RHS Victoria Medal of Honour for his horticultural achievements. Charles Puddle was at the helm when Bodnant Garden was given into the care of the National Trust in 1949. He and his son Martin, who became head gardener in 1982, steered Bodnant through this new era in which it became one of Britain's most famous gardens. The long family link was finally broken when Martin died in 2005.

Above Frederick Puddle

Left Martin (left) and Charles Puddle in 2000

Carrying the baton

The challenge of following in the footsteps of the Puddles was taken up in 2007 by Troy Smith – a former student at Bodnant Garden. Troy drove forward a number of innovations: the renovation of the rose terraces, the redesign and replanting of herbaceous beds and borders and the construction of a new winter garden. He also championed the introduction of volunteer gardeners. Troy left Bodnant Garden in 2013 to take the helm at another National Trust property, Sissinghurst in Kent.

For the following 18 months the ship was steered by Deputy Head Gardener Adam Salvin, who has been a Bodnant gardener, man and boy, since first arriving for work experience as a teenager. Adam led staff and volunteers through a busy period which saw the opening of new areas such as the Yew Dell and Far End, until the arrival of current Head Gardener John Rippin in 2015.

John brings great experience from his career at the famous Hillier Nurseries in Hampshire and the National Trust gardens at Hidcote and Castle Drogo – and brings a new chapter to the story of Bodnant Garden.

Left Taking Bodnant Garden forward in the 21st century: Troy Smith (above) and Adam Salvin (below)

'Seeds and pressed botanical specimens were sent back to the British Isles in tea chests and my grandfather, and father too as a young man, had the excitement of unpacking plants with exotic unknown names that had never been seen in the west before.'

Martin Puddle, Head Gardener, 2003

Right Current Head Gardener John Rippin

The East Garden

Henry Pochin was as passionate about new discoveries in horticulture as in chemistry. He developed the area surrounding Bodnant Hall in formal Victorian fashion and with enormous flair.

He remodelled the existing Georgian house, giving the cream-coloured Italianate frontage an imposing makeover of blue-grey stone. The fine conservatory and fernery attached to Bodnant Hall were built by the leading glasshouse manufacturer of the age, Messenger and Co. Both the house and conservatory remain in the ownership of the donor family.

West of the house Pochin planted two great cedars on the sloping lawn in front of the house, laying the foundations for what was to become the Lily Terrace in the time of his grandson.

Above The Range borders, originally the site of rows of Victorian glasshouses

He also developed the upper East Garden in Italian Renaissance style, its lawns intersected by paths, stone steps and balustrades, and with a terrace linking the house to the garden. Here Pochin planted the specimen conifers he loved – new introductions from foreign lands.

Scientific zeal

The site of the former kitchen garden was transformed into the stately Top Lawn, where Pochin created the Round Garden and The Parterre. A new walled kitchen garden, with rows of glasshouses, was established nearby on the site of the present-day garden centre.

He approached horticulture, and farming too, with a scientific zeal, striving to perfect his fruit and vegetables as well as his crops. *The Manchester Courier* reported in 1888 on 'the great success in the cultivation of pears and apples achieved by Mr Pochin'.

In front of the house he laid the Front Lawn, flanked by beds of tough shrubs suited to the rugged conditions and acidic, clay soil; gaultheria, skimmia, osmanthus and escallonia. There were also decorative beds here, displaying many varieties of nasturtium.

Near the Front Lawn, on the site of a pool created by his predecessor William Hanmer, Pochin introduced an oval pond with terracotta tiled floor in which the family used to bathe, known as The Bath. Water from here was channelled into a stream leading down through the Rockery to the Dell.

In his diary of 1880, Pochin wrote: 'We have finished the bathing pool and the archery' – little knowing that his 'archery' was to become the garden's most famous spectacle.

Right Bodnant Hall seen from across the Front Lawn

The Laburnum Arch

Bodnant Garden's Laburnum Arch is a horticultural marvel. A dazzling 55-metre (60-yard) pergola walkway of golden flowers, it attracts around 50,000 visitors in late May and is the most visited, photographed, talked about and eagerly anticipated sight of the year.

Pergolas were developed during the Renaissance in Mediterranean countries, to provide shelter and shade, and a structure on which to grow vines and fruit. They became popular throughout Europe, falling out of fashion after the 1600s but making a comeback in Victorian times. Henry Pochin decided that he wanted a pergola at Bodnant and, not being a man to do things by halves, he designed his on a grand scale.

The Arch was originally made of the common laburnum variety *Laburnum anagyroides*; these plants were later replaced with the cultivar *Laburnum x watereri 'Vossii'* which produces longer flower racemes and was developed in the 1860s by Waterer's Nursery in Surrey.

There are 48 plants along the length of the Arch; originally these were supported by wooden batons which have now been replaced by a metal frame. There was a yew hedge alongside the walkway but in the 1950s this was removed and replanted with azaleas, creating a colourful flowering backdrop.

Originally there was a glass shade on the wall behind the Arch, with heating pipes at the base, against which tender climbing plants from overseas were grown. A few of the hardiest of these can still be seen today, including some South American specimens.

A labour of love
In January it takes two gardeners up to a month to prune the Arch by hand – painstakingly untying, cutting back and re-tying each strand to the framework – and a further two weeks of work deadheading the flowers in July.

Left A dazzling sight in May and June, the Laburnum Arch

Right Delighting a new generation of visitors today

Victoriana revisited

In the 21st century Henry Pochin's East Garden benefited from improvements under Head Gardener Troy Smith. In 2007 and 2008 the Round Garden and The Parterre were renovated, new paths laid and shrub planting was replaced with perennials, bulbs and box edging.

The derelict glasshouses demolished in the 1980s made way for the Range, a border of hot-coloured grasses and perennial flowers which now glow all summer long and well into autumn.

Nearby, between the Top Lawn and the Laburnum Arch, the Puddle Garden was created. This area pays tribute to head gardeners Frederick, Charles and Martin Puddle and is filled with plants loved by these men, including a number of rhododendron hybrids raised at Bodnant Garden.

The long herbaceous borders of the Front Lawn were renovated by student-gardeners in 2014, refreshing the colourful display of late-flowering perennials. In that year the garden team also began renovating The Bath and surrounding beds, which are now home to a new tropical display of tender and exotic plants.

The Winter Garden

The most spectacular addition to the East Garden has been the Winter Garden – four years in the planning, two years in the making, costing £35,000 to bring to life.

The site was originally a rockery which had become overgrown and was closed to the public. Troy's new design followed the former layout of stone beds, with new paths sinuously sweeping around the plantings. In winter these are lit by the low sunlight shining across the Old Park.

Tall conifers were retained to give structure along with old shrubs such as rhododendrons, garrya, camellia and a stunningly gnarled *Acer palmatum*. Other tall trees were added such as the white birches *Betula utilis* and the silky bronze-barked cherry *Prunus serrula*.

Forming the middle level of the planting scheme are scented shrubs such as witch hazel, daphne and sarcococca, flowering viburnum and camellia, cornus and rubus with their glowing stems, berrying plants such as skimmia, and arching grasses. Layered below this are herbaceous plants including a lovely collection of hellebores and a colourful understorey of bulbs.

The Winter Garden attracted 10,000 visitors in its opening three months in 2013 and is so popular that, instead of closing it to the public in March as originally planned, it now remains open all year.

Far left The Range borders in spring

Left A summer burst of hot colours on The Range

Above Layers of planting provide texture, colour and scent in the new Winter Garden

The Dells and Water Gardens

Bodnant Garden is shaped by water; brooks cascade down the hillside, meeting the River Hiraethlyn which flows through the valley to the River Conwy and the sea.

In the formal upper garden, water has been harnessed into placid ornamental ponds and rivulets over which dragonflies buzz, but through the lower garden it tinkles, crashes and swirls between stream, waterfall, leat and lake. Henry Pochin saw that water defined Bodnant, its terrain and plants, and with his designers Edward and Henry Milner he set out ambitious plans to resculpt the hillside, harnessing nature to create the riverside garden. This came to be known as the Wild Garden.

Work was done in the Yew Dell, Far End and the Dell to reinforce stream and riverbanks preventing erosion; new watercourses were carved and paths were laid to create sinuous cliffside walks, emulating the Welsh hillside rambles of which Pochin was so fond. He was an active superintendent of works, keenly involved in the project and reportedly as knowledgeable as Milner's own foreman.

Land of giants

Trees also define the dells. In Pochin's time, a great wave of tree-planting began in the garden; many American conifers were planted on the east bank of the river in 1876 and on the west bank in 1886. The family continued this tradition into the 1900s as the garden became home to more broad-leaved exotics from Asia.

Right Water defines the lush valley garden

Above Giant conifers provide epic scale in the Pinetum

'The taste of Mr Pochin aided by the skill of his head gardener Mr Saunderson has been directed to the beautifying of the glen ... forming the banks of the stream with slabs of native rock. Rustic bridges, some of wood others simply of rough slabs of stone, cross the main stream and its tributaries and shelter is afforded where some of the paths cross each other by little sheds with thatched roofs, over which honeysuckle grows.'

The Gardeners' Chronicle, 1892

Pochin enjoyed inviting his friends to plant new trees in his garden. He recorded these events in his diaries, including a tree-planting by his friend, the Liberal statesman John Bright, 'who planted on November 18th 1886 a Cedrus Atlantica glauca and a Wellingtonia in the Pinetum'. Some of these saplings are now Champion Trees: they have been officially registered as the biggest and best examples of their kind in the UK. Bodnant Garden has around 40 Champion Trees, many of which are in the dells where they have been sheltered against the elements and have grown taller, reaching for light. There are several other Champions, along with many trees of great age and distinction, around the garden.

The Dell

There are several ways to approach the Dell, all breathtaking. You can, for example, stroll towards it through gently sloping glades and shrub borders, or descend stone steps through the terraces immersed in Italianate splendour. Around a corner a dramatic vista unfolds – a valley of giant trees and a coursing river, swathes of large-leaved plants with brightly coloured flowers illuminating the cool, lush shade.

The Dell runs along the river from the Waterfall Bridge to the Old Mill. Evergreen conifers frame the landscape providing all-year interest while deciduous trees and shrubs provide an unfolding palette through the seasons, all thriving in the moist, shady, acidic conditions.

Unfolding seasons

From winter to early spring dwarf daffodils (*Narcissus cyclamineus*) and snowdrops appear at the feet of the towering trees. Camellias dot the valley sides, among them *Camellia japonica*, introduced to Britain from Asia in the 1700s; *Camellia saluenensis*, discovered by planthunter George Forrest in 1918; and *Camellia x williamsii* hybrids developed by plant breeder John Charles Williams in the 1920s.

In March and April the grand magnolias hold sway, and by May the steep banks are clothed from end to end in a dazzling spectrum of rhododendrons. These range from tall *Rhododendron luteum* with large golden blooms whose scent fill the air, to low and sprawling *Rhododendron japonica* 'Amoena' with its dainty fuchsia-pink flowers – an old type introduced to

Giant Himalayan lily

Originating from the Himalayas the *Cardiocrinum giganteum* was first seen in Britain in the 1850s. It is the largest of the lilies, growing up to 3.5 metres in height. It can take ten years to bloom and needs careful tending, but the enormous scented white flowers are worth the wait.

Above **A visitor's first glimpse of the Dell**

Left **Swathes of Himalayan primulas and hostas on riverbanks**

Top right **The heady scent of *Rhododendron luteum* fills the air in spring**

the UK from Shanghai in 1850 by Robert Fortune. Swathes of Himalayan primulas and poppies, including cerise *Primula pulverulenta* and blue *Meconopsis betonicifolia*, run riot along the riverside mingling with native bluebells.

In summer herbaceous plants come to the fore; hostas, astilbes and ferns – including the large, century-old *Osmunda regalis* – and the giant Himalayan lily makes its star appearance. August brings a display of hydrangeas, notably the electric blue *Hydrangea macrophylla* which line the riverbank. These hold their colour well into autumn, along with the white *Hydrangea paniculata* whose flowers fade to pink and the *Hydrangea quercifolia* with its russet red, oak-like leaves. Japanese acers and the turning colours of deciduous trees produce a glowing canopy throughout autumn in this other-worldly dell.

View from a bridge

Whichever path you take to reach the Dell one of the best places to enjoy the dramatic vista is from the famous Waterfall Bridge.

Henry Pochin rebuilt a dam on the site of an existing pool in order to create a waterfall and enhance the dramatic scenery of the Dell. Here he built a bridge across the river, overlooking the crashing waterfall on one side and the placid Mill Pond on the other. Pochin's bridge was made of larch, complementing other rustic ornamental features dotted through the gorge – small stone bridges and stepping stones, arbours and summerhouses (many now gone). The original bridge was washed away in 1920 and a new one built; it has remained an iconic viewpoint for almost a century.

In 2012 the dam and bridge underwent major renovation when £150,000 was spent on desilting the pond, repairing erosion damage to the dam and replacing bridge timbers.

A river of blue

In summer the riverbank through the Dell is illuminated by electric blue *Hydrangea macrophylla*. Mass planted, the pompom 'mopheads' and feathery 'lacecaps' provide a stunning contrast to their lush green backdrop. The hydrangea blooms, which in other situations would be pink in colour, take on their vibrant blue hue because of the acidic soil in the Dell. Over time they age to greens, mauves and finally bronze, providing three seasons of interest before gardeners prune the thousands of heads in early spring – a task which takes several weeks and many hands.

Far left The Waterfall Bridge

Left The Rockery in spring

The Far End

Beyond the Waterfall Bridge is the Far End, 6.5 hectares (16 acres) of riverside haven very different from the formal terraces and from other 'wild' areas of the garden.

Upstream from the steep-sided Dell the valley opens out; the evergreen conifers don't soar overhead but roll back against the hillside alongside deciduous native and exotic trees – Chinese magnolias and Japanese acers mingling with waterside willows. The river doesn't roar dramatically as it does through the gorge but meanders, via pools and ponds and a lake where birds and even otters can be seen enjoying the calm waters. Here the banks are less manicured; instead they seem to sway with grasses and reeds, and are home to native bogside plants such as loosestrife, spring bulbs and ferns.

Riverside retreat

Originally laid out by Henry Pochin, this area was developed by his daughter Laura as a lakeside retreat where the family enjoyed picnics, fishing, boating and even ice-skating.

The Skating Pond was built in the winter of 1899, diverting water from adjoining fields and brooks which would otherwise flow into the River Hiraethlyn.

At one end of the lake was built an Arts and Crafts-style boathouse with thatched roof, from where the family used to row out to a small island. At its other end is Alder Wood and, in the past, a Chinese-style bridge, long since disappeared.

On the east bank above the Skating Pond is the Serpentine Path which winds through rocky outcrops to join the path to the Yew Dell. Above this is a wider path through an arboretum developed by Laura and Henry McLaren. The McLarens planted many exotic trees here, including the Mexican White Pine (*Pinus ayacahuite*) planted in 1902, which is now a Champion Tree (see page 29).

On the west bank of the Skating Pond is the Williams Bed, 150 metres (164 yards) in length, named after the *Rhododenron williamsianum* which once filled it. These pink flowering rhododendrons were mass-planted in the early 1900s and though none survive there are plans to replace them. Higher up, the Douglas Path leads westwards towards the Dell through a plantation of Douglas fir and other conifers.

Left The river forms pools as it winds through the Far End

Right A place for reflection – Boat House beside the Skating Pond at the Far End

A new lease of life

Above A blaze of leaf colour in autumn

Having remained a private area for more than a century the Far End opened to the public in March 2015, following several years of restoration.

There were many seasons of work for diggers clearing the silted-up pools and ponds, for arborists removing sickly old trees and for gardeners and volunteers renovating banks, beds and paths. The Williams Bed was in need of major renovation; dead or unhealthy trees and shrubs were removed, others had to be pruned hard back, weeds and brambles were cleared and the whole bed mulched. New plants introduced included Himalayan types like the blue *Meconopsis grandis* 'Lingholm' and *Primula prolifera* with its yellow and violet flowers. The great wood-rush (*Luzula sylvatica*) was mass planted extensively to retain the riverbanks and throughout the area new plantings included perennials such as iris, poppies and primulas, and shrubs for all-year colour.

Alder Wood underwent the most dramatic work, with drainage added, a new bridge built and new pathway made to give visitors a level, accessible circular route around the lake. Gardeners removed invasive bamboo and replanted the area with ornamental trees, grasses and waterside herbaceous plants.

In 2014 the boathouse underwent extensive renovation. Contractors replaced damaged wood with Welsh oak and were able to source the same Cornish roof tiles which had replaced the earlier thatch in 1938.

A battle with nature

The renovation wasn't without setbacks – the floods of winter 2011 caused extensive damage, sweeping away new riverside plantings and tearing up paths – but the work continued, the ropes finally came down and a new generation of visitors is now enjoying this tranquil riverside retreat.

The opening of the Far End was celebrated with a grand ceremony, at which horticultural broadcaster Christine Walkden sheared a ceremonial ribbon and Garden Director Michael McLaren gave a speech on behalf of Bodnant Garden's donor family.

The Far End is now a perfect area for nature lovers – for walking, birdwatching, photography, or simply sitting. It's a welcoming place for families, where children can get closer to nature by den building, pond dipping and bug-hunting in the picnic area. The lakeside is also a flat and level garden area accessible for those with limited mobility.

Above The Skating Pond on a bright spring day

Left Himalayan poppies have made their home on waterside beds

The Yew Dell

Named after the yew trees which still hold sway there, the name of this little wooded glade doesn't hint at the horticultural history packed into its 1.4 hectares (3.5 acres), which contain some of Bodnant's oldest and rarest plants.

Formerly a quarry cliff leading down to a swampy area, it was claimed for the garden by Henry Pochin who laid out the streamside paths and planted the yews, and drifts of snowdrops, hyacinth, daffodils and *Chionodoxa*, in the style of a 'wild garden' alongside The Dell and Far End.

Another metamorphosis occurred from the 1900s when Pochin's grandson Henry McLaren began filling the Yew Dell with rhododendrons brought back from the plant-hunting expeditions of Ernest Wilson, George Forrest and Frank Kingdon-Ward.

A secret garden

In the years that followed the Yew Dell became home to many Bodnant hybrid rhododendrons, serving as a nursery for these special plants, but remained closed to the public, untouched apart from basic management. It has thus developed a uniquely secluded, lush atmosphere – part Himalayan glade, part native woodland, part bog, with mature rhododendrons and hydrangeas overhung by oak, ash and magnolia.

The Yew Dell was opened to the public in 2014 after renovation by gardeners and volunteers which involved weeding, cutting back brambles and pruning shrubs and trees, as well as repairing paths and drains. Plants have been added, including hydrangea, euonymus and acer to extend interest into autumn. The rhododendron collection has also been expanded.

Right A carpet of rhododendron blossom beneath trees in the Yew Dell

Left The tree-sized *Rhododendron ririei* in the Yew Dell is believed to have been grown from seed collected in China by Ernest Wilson in 1917, making it a century old. It's one of the earlier rhododendrons, evergreen with large lilac flowers in February

Skunk cabbage

In spring the Yew Dell is illuminated by masses of *Lysichiton americanus*. Introduced to Britain at the turn of the 1900s, this herbaceous plant is striking in appearance (and scent), with glossy oval leaves up to a metre long and bright yellow arum-like flowers. Love or hate them, they have become part of the landscape in Bodnant's boggy dells. EU rules now ban new plantings and here at Bodnant Garden they are managed to prevent their spread.

'A picturesque cliff reclaimed for horticultural purposes and now thickly planted with Chinese primulas amidst a profusion of rhododendrons ... not only every Chinese, Himalayan and American species introduced into this country; not only every first rate hybrid, but great numbers of all the best ... a limitless gallery of beauty.'

The Gardeners' Chronicle, 1928

Rare rhododendrons

Bodnant Garden is world famous for its rhododendrons and the Yew Dell is home to many of the garden's oldest. Among them are special ones unique to the garden: the Bodnant hybrids.

Rhododendrons began trickling into Britain during the 1700s from Europe, America and the Near East. The trickle became a flow from the late 1800s with new discoveries in China and Japan. From the turn of the 1900s Henry McLaren began sponsoring plant-hunting expeditions which generated a new wave of rhododendrons to Britain, and to Bodnant Garden.

Legend has it that the head gardener at the time at first didn't believe they would be hardy enough to grow in North Wales. Thankfully he was proved wrong. They acclimatised so well that Bodnant Garden went on to develop a highly successful plant-breeding programme collecting numerous awards and gold medals at national flower shows.

Above The Yew Dell; once a 'swampy place', it is now home to many old, rare and hybrid rhododendrons

Opposite clockwise from top left Bodnant Hybrids, *Rhododendron* 'Adonis' and 'Elizabeth', and the species *Rhododendron cinnabarinium*

New hues

Many of the early rhododendrons offered an entirely new colour palette and range of genes with which to work. Those that were planted at Bodnant included *Rhododendron wardii* (the first strong yellow), *Rhododendron cinnabarinum* (which introduced orange shades), and the 'Bodnant Bloody Reds' for which the garden became so famous, including *Rhododendron forrestii* and *Rhododendron griersonianum*.

One aim of hybridisation was to extend the flowering season by using early and late flowering species; also to produce stronger plants by crossing tender plants with more hardy species. Another motive was to produce smaller plants suitable for the domestic market, the most famous example of this being *Rhododendron* 'Elizabeth' named after Henry's eldest child. It is still one of the most popular rhododendrons in the UK.

In 2015 these unique, Bodnant-bred plants were granted Plant Heritage status as a new National Collection, reflecting Bodnant Garden's place in the great British history of rhododendrons.

Near extinction

More than 300 hybrid rhododendrons were raised and registered to Bodnant Garden. To date there are only 115 known varieties in the garden and some exist only as a single specimen. Some plants have died out; others are thought to be still in the garden but have lost their labels. The garden team has been working with metal detectorists to help locate the missing plant labels. Gardeners are also actively propagating some of the 'at risk' hybrids and plan to restart a Bodnant Garden hybridisation programme in the future.

The Glades

Fanning out south-west of the garden is an informal area linking the ordered Italianate terraces to the craggy, wild dells – grassy glades providing the garden's best seasonal panoramas and shrub borders of dappled shade.

Pastoral drifts

Beyond the manicured lawns of the upper East Garden a new vista emerges. Grass glades running alongside the Old Park to the Yew Dell roll out through the seasons in a carpet of snowdrops, daffodils, bluebells and other wildflowers – begun by nature and enhanced by generations of gardeners, who continue every year adding to the display. This area evolved in the 1920s when Henry McLaren began cultivating the old parkland by planting bulbs and specimen trees.

Today, Japanese cherries, flowering crab apples and magnolias provide a canopy of blossom in spring while the fruit, berry and leaf colour of ash, oak, rowan, cornus, and scented *Cercydiphyllum japonicum*, give a fiery autumn display. At the top of Chapel Park is the Acer Glade, which glows red, purple and gold in October, and gives a tantalising glimpse of the Poem through the trees.

The Poem

Sited on a rocky outcrop overlooking the Dell, this Grade II-listed building was created by Henry Pochin in 1882 as a final resting place for the children he and Agnes lost in infancy, and for themselves and their descendants.

The Poem was designed by architects W.J. Green of London, the marble interior sculpted by Samuel Barfield of Leicester, and the stained glass windows shaped like snowflakes were designed by Pochin himself. Mystery surrounds the name of the building, which is believed to stand for 'place of eternal memory'.

The famous landscape gardeners, James Pulham and Sons, who pioneered the use of Pulhamite, an artificial stone for grottoes and rock gardens, had already worked on the conservatory at Bodnant Hall. The firm was called in again to sculpt great 'outcrops' which supported the chapel and added to the picturesque scenery.

This rockery was planted with heathers and is surrounded by mature conifers and broad-leaved trees, camellias, rhododendrons and other large shrubs. In 1904 a series of terraces were added in front of the Poem; the planting of these was redesigned by one of Bodnant's student-gardeners in 2008 on the theme of an ethereal white garden.

The building was restored in 1970 and 2007 and is now open to visitors periodically through the summer.

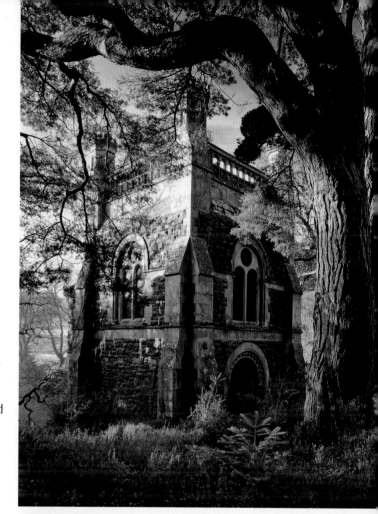

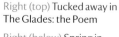

Left **Autumn colour in Chapel Park**

Right (top) Tucked away in The Glades: the Poem

Right (below) Spring in The Glades and daffodils as far as the eye can see

A home for exotics

Alongside the grassy glades is an area of shrub borders. It was originally the site of long herbaceous beds set out by Pochin and his daughter Laura which, according to family records, 'never did well'. This area came into its own under Henry McLaren who planted new trees and shrubs brought back from his plant-hunting expeditions. Fine examples of specimens from Bodnant Garden's five National Collections can be seen here.

Old Hanmer's Pool near The Bath marks the gateway to these shrub borders and in spring it's unmissable, with a dazzling display of rhododendrons and candelabra-type primroses, *Primula pulverulenta*, first introduced to Britain by Ernest Wilson. From here a gravel path leads past a towering *Sequoiadendron giganteum* (planted in 1875) to borders lined with many Chinese trees and shrubs providing spring blossom and autumn leaf and berry colour: *Cornus kousa chinensis*, *Styrax hemsleyana*, *Viburnum plicatum*, stewartia, camellia, enkianthus, forsythia and *corylopsis* overhanging beds of hydrangeas, gallica roses and herbaceous perennials. Planthunter Wilson is evident again in the peeling-barked *Acer griseum* and most famously in the *Davidia involucrata* (Handkerchief tree).

5

1

2

National Collections

(1) *Rhododendron forrestii* and its hybrids – Collected by George Forrest on his first expedition to China in 1905. It is a low-growing plant with large, bright red flowers and glossy deep-green leaves.

(2) Rhododendron hybrids raised at Bodnant Garden – More than 300 hybrids were raised and registered to Bodnant Garden, including the *Rhododendron* 'Charles Aberconway' (pictured).

(3) Magnolia species – The garden is home to many Chinese magnolias dating from the plant-hunting expeditions of Wilson, Forrest and others. When the famous Veitch Nursery closed in 1914, Henry McLaren reputedly bought up the stock and commissioned a train to deliver it to Bodnant – some of these now mature trees can be seen in the Glades and on the Magnolia Walk.

(4) Embothrium species and its hybrids – Specimens of the Chilean firebush collected by Harold Comber during his Andes expeditions of the 1920s can be seen throughout the Glades and Dells. The *Embothrium coccineum* (pictured) is a large, suckering shrub or tree with evergreen leaves and dense bunches of brilliant-red flowers in June.

(5) Eucryphia species and its hybrids – Also collected by Comber, these small trees from South America produce creamy-white, scented flowers in late summer. The deciduous *Eucryphia glutinosa* can be seen in the upper Glades, while *Eucryphia x intermedia* 'Rostrevor' is on the Magnolia Walk.

The handkerchief tree

Ernest Wilson searched China for this tree, first spotted by the Irish missionary and botanist, Augustine Henry, who had marked the spot with an X on a piece of paper covering some 20,000 square miles of land. Against the odds Wilson did find it.

Back in Britain the seeds he had procured were sown by Veitch Nursery, but thrown out onto a compost heap after failing to grow. A year later seedlings appeared in the compost. Bodnant Garden's trees are believed to have come from this original, rescued batch of seedlings – which we now know are particularly slow to germinate.

The Terraces

Today Bodnant Garden is world famous for its five Italianate terraces, built between 1904 and 1914. They were designed by Henry McLaren and his mother Laura, who also designed the garden terraces at the Grade II-listed Golden Grove nearby in Flintshire.

Faced with an 'uninteresting' lawn, Henry McLaren drew inspiration from the two great cedars planted there by his grandfather Henry Pochin, planning the entire layout of the terraces around them.

Over the course of a decade five beautiful terraces were carved out of the grassy hillside which sloped westward from Bodnant Hall to the River Hiraethlyn. They were filled with rose beds, pergolas of climbing wisteria and clematis, fountains, rivulets and lily pools and billowing herbaceous borders, each offering stunning views of the Carneddau Mountains beyond.

Top Bodnant Garden's west lawn after the construction of the terraces

Right The sloping west lawn of Bodnant Garden before the terraces were built

'My mother loved flowers and I loved first of all flowering shrubs and we thought it out together. We drew a plan of terraces on one of the lawns, a lawn sloping west, a wind-swept and rather bare lawn, very dignified but I confess most uninteresting.'

Henry McLaren, 1950

A lasting legacy

The terraces are a testament to the vision of the garden's founder family and to the men who built them, some of whom went away to fight in the First World War and did not return.

This massive earth moving project was done by men with wheelbarrows and carts. Granite was quarried from the surrounding estate to build great buttressed walls which provided shelter for the exotic new plants such as the Chinese magnolias. It is estimated that the amount of work done by 50 labourers in one hour before the First World War would equate to that of one skilled labourer using machinery after the Second World War.

The project employed scores of estate groundsmen, gardeners and general labourers, as well as 'journeymen' – travelling carpenters, builders and stonemasons – who lodged with village families.

The toll of war on a small community was immense and cut across social boundaries. Many of the 22 men named on the war memorial in the nearby village of Eglwysbach lived and worked at Bodnant – among them Thomas Owen, the garden nursery apprentice, and Eric Saunderson, son of the retired head gardener. Listed alongside them is Francis McLaren, Laura's younger son, a young politician full of promise.

In 2014 the BBC visited Bodnant Garden to film the series *Glorious Gardens from Above*, when a commemorative urn was being installed in the lower rose terrace pergola. It was inscribed with the Welsh words Nefoedd ar Ddaear, 'Heaven on Earth'. The urn marks the centenary of the garden terraces and the outbreak of the First World War.

Left Lord and Lady Aberconway's younger son Francis was killed in the First World War, along with 21 other young men from the village and estate

The Top Rose Terrace

This first and highest of the five terraces overlooks a breathtaking panorama of the Carneddau Mountains.

There are two rows of rose beds lined with saxifrage, campanula and rock roses. In borders alongside, tall *Lilium regale* add to the summer display and *Verbena bonariensis* billows into the autumn. Two of the oldest inhabitants of this terrace, planted around 1906, are the Strawberry Trees (*Arbutus x andrachnoides*) with their eye-catching glossy pink bark and gnarled trunks. Nearby is the heliochronometer, a precision sundial dating back to around 1910.

Overlooking the terrace are two sphinxes bought by Henry McLaren in 1936 (there are two more of these on the Lower Rose Terrace) and a classical statue depicting Bacchus, a god of fertility.

The Top Rose Terrace was renovated in 2006 and the Lower Rose Terrace in 2012 when ageing hybrid tea roses were replaced by David Austin New English Roses, providing a long display from June to October.

The Croquet Terrace

Wisteria venusta and *Wisteria floribunda* tumble down wide steps leading to the Croquet Terrace. At the base of the steps is a French Baroque fountain, made around 1700 by Bouchardin and brought to Bodnant in 1940. The long, curving wall was built to provide protection for tender plants such as the grand *Magnolia campbellii subsp. mollicomata* (one of planthunter Forrest's finds), now more than a century old, which produces

large, saucer-shaped pink flowers. The long lawn in front of these beds provides the perfect spot for games of croquet, still enjoyed by visitors today.

The Lily Terrace

Across the croquet lawn is a long, balustrade wall overlooking the mountain vista and further steps leading down to the Lily Terrace. Taking centre stage here is the Lily Pond, with towering blue *Cedrus atlantica glauca* and *Cedrus libani* planted by Henry Pochin at either end.

An ornamental vine, *Vitis coignetiae*, cascades down the back buttressed wall, which supports tender shrubs like *Schima argentea*, *Eucryphia lucida* and a large *Magnolia delavayi* (a Wilson discovery) which was recorded in *The Garden* magazine of 1915 as being the first to flower that year. The bays in between the buttresses are home to mass displays of hydrangeas which are a vibrant colour spectacle through summer and autumn.

On either side of the pond are beds of Bodnant hybrid rhododendrons, planted in 2014. Set against that mountain view is a long herbaceous border which flowers pastel pink and lavender all summer, billowing with ornamental grasses well into winter.

Left **Top Rose Terrace in summer**

Above **View of the house from the Lily Terrace**

The Lower Rose Terrace

Paths through a clipped yew hedge on the Lily Terrace lead to a walkway lined with swaying angels' fishing rods (*Dierama pulcherrimum*). This is the ideal place to look down through the labyrinth of Arts and Crafts-style pergolas which burst into colour from spring onwards with clematis, wisteria, roses and other climbers, including a mature *Magnolia grandiflora* 'Goliath'. Here is also the spot to view the pergola urns, copied from a design in the loggia of London's Ritz Hotel.

More stone steps wind past the Libertia Walk, and open out onto the Lower Rose Terrace. Here rectangular beds of roses mingle with salvias, lilies and agapanthus. At the north end of the Terrace is the herbaceous Pink Garden, and beyond that the Yucca Garden, with exotic planting including euphorbias, acanthus and crocosmia. At the south end is the White Garden, designed by one of Bodnant Garden's students in 2013, where an old *Rosa gardenia* spills down the wall in summer. Just beyond this is the new Gentian Bed containing rare and unusual woodland plants, and a Poppy Bed of Himalayan species, both created in 2015.

Below Sphinx statue on the Lower Rose Terrace

The Canal Terrace

In a grand finale, the Lower Rose Terrace opens out onto the Canal Terrace with its long pond flanked by herbaceous beds. In 2015 and 2016, while awaiting renovation, these were planted up as temporary wildflower borders providing a stunning summer display. At the north end of the pond is the Stage, a platform of clipped yews designed in 18th-century Italian style. The classical seat is based on a design by William Kent (another can be seen on the Lily Terrace).

The Pin Mill

Dating from 1730, the Pin Mill was built at Woodchester in Gloucestershire where it is believed to have been a hunting lodge, then a mill for the manufacture of pins and finally a tannery. In 1938 after a local appeal to restore the derelict building failed Henry McLaren bought it and had his estate workers dismantle and move it brick-by-brick to Bodnant Garden.

At first he intended to rebuild it in the centre of the terrace but was persuaded by his wife Christabel and son Charles that it would be better at one end, so it could be reflected in the Canal Pond.

The Pin Mill houses a ground-floor gallery and an upstairs panelled room which the family used as a music room and summerhouse. The building underwent major restoration in 2013. The gallery hosts visiting musicians on Sunday afternoons and the upstairs room is open through the summer months.

In July white and pink water lilies adorn the Canal Pond and Lily Pond. They also provide launch pads for thousands of froglets in June, making their way from the water to the safety of nearby undergrowth. Bodnant's gardeners have fashioned wildlife ramps to help amphibians, insects, stray birds and mammals clamber out of the ponds.

Above The Lower Rose Terrace, Canal Terrace and Pin Mill

The North Garden

At the furthest end of the Top Rose Terrace is an alpine bed. Designed by one of Bodnant's gardeners in 2011 and sheltered by a terrace wall, it contains many rare, dwarf rock garden gems.

Beyond this a network of snaking paths leads to the North Garden – home to mature native oak, beech and yew, along with exotic introductions such as *Athrotaxis selaginoides*, *Acer griseum*, *Magnolia denudata* and *Magnolia robusta*. Here too are many large old rhododendrons which have attained the stature of small trees.

A sloping lawn is lined with beds containing many shrubby species rhododendrons, including the orange *Rhododendron cinnabarinum*, blood red *Rhododendron barbatum*, deciduous types like *Rhododendron albrechtii*, *Rhododendron schlippenbachii*, *Rhododendron augustinii* and some rare specimens of the creamy-white *Rhododendron* 'Penjerrick' from the garden of the same name in Cornwall.

The rhododendron beds replaced numerous Lawson cypresses planted in Pochin's day. Some of the work was done by prisoners of war interned at nearby camps during the First World War and the area has since become known as the German Beds. Beyond the cultivated garden is Cae Poeth Meadow, a wildflower-rich grassland.

Right The sweeping lawn of the North Garden

The Primula Path

The North Garden has undergone considerable work in recent years. Large trees have fallen victim to storm damage and shrubs have succumbed to poor health and old age, but this has given our gardeners the opportunity to create new paths and replant beds.

Renovations have included the opening of the Primula Path, an old walkway bordering the North Garden which was closed to the public for many years. It opened in 2014, with repaired wall and pathway, and new beds planted with Himalayan primulas and poppies which provide a mass of colour in late spring.

Past and Present

During the 1800s there were several moods in British gardening which influenced Bodnant Garden's design, interweaving the wild and formal, the native and exotic, the old and new.

In the first half of that century John Claudius Loudon was at the forefront of a Gardenesque style which brought back a horticultural wow factor to the 'natural' parkland of the Georgian era. As the Empire expanded and curious new plants arrived from abroad, garden owners like Henry Pochin created beds, rockeries and glasshouses in which to grow them – and show them off – to perfection.

These developments were fed by advances in botany, transport and manufacturing; as a by-product they brought gardens to the masses. There was a blossoming of public parks and arboreta where people could marvel at bright bedding plants and trees from foreign lands.

Back to nature

Alongside the march of industry was a yearning for a return to nature and a simpler, rural past – expressed by the Romantic poets, painters and philosophers of the early 1800s, by the Pre-Raphaelite artists who followed on and by the designers of the Arts and Crafts movement at the century's close.

There was a desire for the homespun in horticulture too. Writer James Shirley Hibberd championed the rise of suburban gardens, but went beyond bedding schemes, advising amateurs how to grow vegetables, how to keep bees and fish, and how to encourage garden birds. His 1856 book *Rustic Adornments for Homes of Taste* led to a boom in the popularity of summer houses and shelters.

William Robinson bucked the Victorian trend for exotic hothouse gardening. In his book *The Wild Garden* of 1870 he encouraged planting which suited the climate, soil and terrain, blending trees and shrubs, perennials and bulbs in informal drifts.

Left The Dell at the turn of the 19th century

Glasshouses, summerhouses and garden rooms

A man of science and industry, Henry Pochin embraced horticultural advances – building greenhouses, growing exotic plants and using artificial stone. With a commitment to education, he was inviting groups of visitors to view his gardens from an early date. At the same time, his decision to plant a collection of conifers in the Dell shows his botanical understanding of their growing needs, and an artistic appreciation of the picturesque scene they would create. The naturalistic planting and rustic adornments in Pochin's valley garden show influences of both Robinson and Hibberd.

At the beginning of the 1900s there was a revival in formal garden design. This found its ultimate expression in the partnership of Arts and Crafts architect Sir Edwin Lutyens, and Gertrude Jekyll. The terraces created by Laura and Henry McLaren – with their carefully designed steps, stone paths, pergolas and garden rooms, and the exuberant planting of roses, herbaceous plants and flowering shrubs – were a personal celebration of this new Edwardian style.

Above Italianate formality, flowing planting and intimate garden rooms on the terraces, 1920s

An ever-changing garden

For more than 200 years Bodnant Garden has been continually evolving. It has embodied many styles – from Georgian naturalism to Victorian grandeur and thence to Edwardian romance, maturing through the 20th century into a world-class garden.

In the 21st century gales, frosts, floods, disease and the passage of time have taken their natural toll. The years from 2007 saw challenges and dynamic change under Head Gardener Troy Smith and his successor John Rippin. New life has been given to old and ailing beds – some

Below The garden is now popular with dog walkers at certain times

Right Wilder areas are a place for fun and discovery for families

refreshed, others remodelled – embracing new ideas while staying true to the unique character of Bodnant Garden.

A New Age

Tastes have changed; visitors appreciate not just the carefully cultivated but also the natural and the 'work in progress'. At Bodnant Garden this has spurred efforts to open once-private areas to the public: the Winter Garden in 2012, Old Park in 2013, the Yew Dell in 2014 and Far End in 2015. Furnace Hill and Meadow, the Heather Hill and Cae Poeth Meadow are still to come.

As the world becomes increasingly high-tech there's also a deepening urge to reconnect with nature. In recent years Bodnant Garden has developed new refreshment kiosks and toilets, play areas for children, picnic areas, welcome days for dog walkers and an events calendar to make the garden an experience which can be enjoyed by a whole new generation of visitors.

Above all, efforts will go on to ensure that Bodnant Garden remains a horticultural jewel in the crown of the National Trust, 'For Ever, For Everyone'.

'No garden is ever finished. Either additions and growth exceed decay so that a garden soars to even greater heights of beauty, or in the course of a mere brute struggle for existence, between plant and plant, it reverts gradually to wilderness.'

Frank Kingdon-Ward, planthunter

The Bath and Vanessa Beds

Bordering the Front Lawn, this bed is named after the *Rhododendron* 'Vanessa' hybrids originally planted there. The area was renovated by student-gardeners in 2014 and 2015 after winter storms brought down a 200-year-old oak. A new section of lawn was laid which now gives a view across the garden and of a large, formerly overshadowed, weeping birch. Beds were redesigned and replanted for all-year interest. Nearby, The Bath (pictured) was transformed into an exotic poolside garden which opened in 2016.

Phoenix rising: Furnace Hill

Furnace Hill, like many areas of Bodnant Garden, has been through challenges and changes. What began life as a hillside dotted with native trees was transformed from 1895 by Laura McLaren who began planting Douglas and Corsican firs, larch and numerous Californian pines. She also established a shelter belt of birch and pine and the spreading woodland *Rhododendron ponticum*. Her son Henry went on to add Asian rhododendrons.

Lying on the fringes of the estate, Furnace Hill remained private for many decades. In recent years the garden team has been renovating the area ready for its public unveiling in 2017.

Sudden Oak Death

Furnace Hill and other wooded areas of the garden have been at the centre of a 21st-century battle to eradicate the disease *Phytophthora ramorum* (Greek for 'plant destroyer'). At the heart of that battle has been *Rhododendron ponticum*. This familiar purple-flowered rhododendron was introduced to Britain in the late 1700s, probably from the Mediterranean, and became popular in the Victorian era when it appeared in parks and gardens. In recent years it was found to be a host for *Phytophthora* – first identified in the United States as Sudden Oak Death. Making its way to Britain the disease began to affect a variety of native and exotic trees and shrubs. It reached Bodnant in the last decade where it targeted some of the garden's ornamental specimens such as viburnums.

Working with DEFRA (Department for Environment, Food and Rural Affairs) the team has been removing *Rhododendron ponticum* and other host species such as larch, rigorously testing trees and shrubs and removing unhealthy plants. In 2015 the garden was granted a clean bill of health. In-house monitoring continues and while some old characters in the garden's landscape have been lost, the spaces left behind have given gardeners the opportunity to plant anew.

Penjerrick Walk

The renovation of Furnace Hill has included the restoration of Penjerrick Walk. This avenue of creamy-white hybrid *Rhododendron* 'Penjerrick' was planted by Henry McLaren. The plants in this area died out over the years – although some specimens remain in the North Garden. With help from the Rhododendron, Camellia and Magnolia Group of the RHS, Bodnant Garden has been able to micro-propagate plant material at a specialist laboratory in Duchy College, Cornwall. Young shrubs were planted out in Furnace Hill in 2015, at a lower spot on the hillside where it's hoped they will now thrive.

Left Native and exotic trees on Furnace hillside

A gardener's work

Gardeners work all year in all weathers to maintain and develop the garden, supported by volunteers and students of horticulture. As the ground warms up in spring, the team starts weeding, mulching beds with homemade compost, planting and pruning shrubs (including a mass pruning of hydrangeas) and clearing away acres of fallen blossom. Other big jobs of the spring are deadheading daffodils in the Old Park and weeding the slopes of the Dell – which has to be done by gardeners trained in abseiling.

With warmer, longer days of summer the garden is at its peak and the team are busy deadheading roses, feeding and watering flower borders, cutting and shaping box hedges, summer pruning laburnum and wisteria and mowing both the manicured lawns and the grassy glades.

As the leaves turn, gardeners turn their attention to scarifying lawns and renovating turf, tidying herbaceous displays and planting spring bulbs. The end of the season brings the mammoth task of collecting 32 hectares (80 acres) of leaves, which go onto the compost heaps. While many gardens are 'put to bed' in winter there's still plenty to do at Bodnant; pruning roses, tree surgery, re-gravelling paths, repairing drains, fixing rabbit fences and pruning the Laburnum Arch. Big team efforts go into planting snowdrops 'in the green' – around 20,000 each February – and mucking out the streams which run from top to bottom of the garden.

'I've been lucky enough to work with both the 3rd Lord Aberconway and with Head Gardener Martin Puddle in the 1980s and 1990s. There have been massive changes in that time but to me the garden is as magical now as it has always been. This place is who I am.'

Mark Morris, Gardener, 2016

Left Watering the Yucca Garden in summer

Top Gardener Mark Morris (left) with an assistant laying hardcore

Above Pruning hydrangeas along riverbanks in the Dell in winter

Green shoots

Students come from across the UK and abroad to train with the team at Bodnant Garden, gaining academic qualifications and hands-on skills. The garden welcomes students of all ages and backgrounds; they help with every aspect of daily work and give enthusiasm and commitment in spades. Over the years the garden has cast its spell on many of them who have returned later as qualified gardeners – including former Head Gardener Troy Smith.

A team effort

Each year more than 200,000 visitors come to Bodnant Garden from across the UK and overseas. Greeting all those people are the Visitor Services team – providing a welcome in the reception, keeping the tills ticking over in the shop and hot drinks flowing in the tearooms. The team includes behind-the-scenes maintenance staff and an office supporting the whole operation.

Volunteers

Volunteers are the lifeblood of Bodnant Garden and around 120 people give their free time to help in a variety of ways.

Garden volunteers play a huge part, working alongside the gardeners in a range of daily tasks and providing extra muscle for large jobs such as planting snowdrops in spring and clearing leaves in autumn. The support of volunteers has also made it possible to renovate and open new areas like the Yew Dell, Far End and the Winter Garden.

Visitor Services volunteers are just as active, every day of the week, meeting and greeting visitors, giving guided tours, staffing car parks and assisting with family activities like pond dipping. They turn their hands to just about everything and anything that comes along, whether it's providing First Aid to injured wildlife or helping reunite lost children with parents. They have also been responsible for driving forward new initiatives such as renovating the Old Mill in the Dell for use as an eating area and events venue.

A vital part of the team are the visitors, who come in their hundreds of thousands each year. Their love of the garden pours out in the comment cards and through the pictures shared on social media every week, and provides continued inspiration to Bodnant Garden's staff and volunteers; crucially, their support helps the National Trust maintain this and many other of our nation's special places.

Left Helping set up a textile exhibition at the garden – one of many roles for Visitor Services volunteers

Below Gardeners, volunteers and visitors in a scything workshop at Cae Poeth Meadow

The future

I do hope that you have enjoyed your visit to my family's garden. My own love for this place is deep in my DNA. I know of no other garden like it – striking contrasts and dramatic landscapes combined with sublime beauty, peace and tranquillity. Nature's steep slopes, abundant water and imposing mountain backdrop have provided a fertile canvas for man's addition of formal terraces and lawns. Their juxtaposition with the more informal shrub borders and parkland, framed in turn by the wild Dell and the sylvan Far End beyond, is both inspired and inspiring.

Yet challenges abound. Not just external challenges, like climate change – but also internal challenges, such as keeping Bodnant fresh and vibrant. The garden was created because generations of gardeners thought outside the box, undertook daring projects (the terraces) and tried novel plants (new introductions). So we, the current custodians, cannot rest on our laurels. We owe it to Bodnant, to my forebears and to our visitors to remain dynamic and imaginative; to continue to incorporate the best of new plants and ideas; and not to shy away from major improvements.

Bodnant must remain a place of horticultural education and inspiration in garden design, as my grandfather envisaged. In this, horticultural excellence coupled with the preservation of the beauty and tranquillity of Bodnant will be our top priority, so as to enhance the enjoyment of all visitors to the garden.

Please return soon; we will always have new plantings or projects to share with you. But in any case, the garden varies greatly between different seasons, and from year to year. Despite having known it for over 50 years, Bodnant never ceases to surprise and delight me – on any walk, I know that I shall see something new which I had never seen before and that I shall be enchanted afresh.

Michael McLaren

Above Swathes of late winter snowdrops herald a new year beginning again at Bodnant Garden